To:
my dear St
Aune Ste

Thank you for
your support

Yours S. Name

. . . . 11-04-1981

Tamara S. Nance

iUniverse, Inc.
New York   Bloomington

11-04-81

iUniverse books may be ordered through booksellers or by contacting:

*iUniverse
1663 Liberty Drive
Bloomington, IN 47403
www.iuniverse.com
1-800-Authors (1-800-288-4677)*

*Because of the dynamic nature of the Internet, any Web addresses or
links contained in this book may have changed since publication and
may no longer be valid. The views expressed in this work are solely those
of the author and do not necessarily reflect the views of the publisher,
and the publisher hereby disclaims any responsibility for them.*

ISBN: 978-1-4502-3318-7 (sc)
ISBN: 978-1-4502-3320-0 (ebook)
ISBN: 978-1-4502-3319-4 (dj)

Printed in the United States of America

iUniverse rev. date: 6/22/2010

Contents

Introduction

This manuscript is to explore the first 18 years my life. When I look back and read the book myself. I find the first 18 years of my life amazing. I was amaze to know that I survived each event that occurred. I had witness many awful things in my life. I wanted to be completely honesty and bring them to the forefront. I was also very sincere when writing this book. I realize in my writing that I was discussing people who I really cared about. I had been through many trials and tribulations which had cause me to endure a lot of pain. I wasn't able to communicate this pain in a proper manner. I became withdrawal from people, had low self-esteem, and little confidence because I endure so much pain. This pain has caused me to ruin relationship with some of my dearest friends. I just needed healing and I apologize to who I have hurt in the past. I have overcome all of this pain I grew older and closer to God. In writing this book I came to my inner peace with all my trials and tribulations. I knew that God was holding my hand the whole way and this is how I maintain through my life. I once was bitter, angry, and sad but now I had forgiven everybody including myself. I now know that having these negative emotions is poison to my well being. I will just pray for everybody that has every cause me pain. I pray for everyone I have hurt as well. I know now to stay focus, have forgiveness, and praying is the keys to a success life. Thank you for your support to whom read this book. I hope the book bring you and revelation to know that even though we experience hardship. We can overcome anything through the grace of God. Some of this book contents in this book has been modified.

Acknowledgement

My family has been the main source of my survival. Our family is very close and we talk to one another about the good and the bad. We are very honest with one another. I appreciate my family support throughout the years. There have been key sufficient people in my family who has been their no matter what. My sister (Redd or my red baby) has been my rock my whole entire life. All our lives we have had each other when we didn't have nobody else. Our bond is unbelievable close. She is the only person on this earth that totally understand me and vice versa. I have to thank her for everything she has done. I am truly blessed to have a little sister like her. I would like to acknowledge my grandmothers' next. My grandmother Evenlyn past away from the complications of Lupus at the age of 54 years old But, she instills the spirit of God in me before she went. My grandmother Mattie just passed away this year of the loving age of 84. She instill in me the will of God, how to be independent, and to never give up. My mother I learned how to have a heart, cook, clean and how to communicate. My Aunt J is the strongest woman I ever seen in my life. She battle Lupus and still maintain to go to work on a daily basis. When her Lupus flares up her she still tell you that she okay and don't worry. She ensures us she will be here for a while because of her strength and will to live. She instilled in me structure and strength. My cousin Hank, brother Quan a cousin K.D. all our brothers because that how we grew up I appreciate them for giving me the key to how men are. They are very supportive as well. When I need someone to talk about a male they are as was there. My cousin Ray who has been a brother as well you always give me advice and you have such much love in your heart for your family I really admire that. My cousin Raheeem Kyree Ford (Uncle Pumpkin son) who always kept the family together and never had nothing bad to say about anybody. He passed away on May 16, 2010 from a brain tumor. You are truly missed. He set the tone for all the grandchildren because he was the oldest grandchild on my father side of the family. I cherish you for your grace and peaceful demeanor. My father this is a man of great unique character features who has supported me all through college and beyond. Whenever I need him he there whether it money or someone to talk too. He is a very easy to talk to he give advice in his own special way. I admire each of them for their different strength, talents, and abilities. To my younger sibling who I love dearly Lawonna, Willie, Mike (my little cousin who like a bother) and Tamari and Tamia. My entire younger sibling you give me strength. I have to pay tribute to a host of female cousins; Ebonie Thomas who heart is pure as gold, Donecia Smith who is very mild manner and sweet, Laneice Smith who is very fun, loving and kind. Devere Green who is very real and always there no matter what, Anitra Green is very fun to be around, you keep me laughing. I love all of you and thanks for the support throughout the years. My whole family has given strength I didn't know I had. You guys always make me feel special, and bring so much joy in my life thank you.

Chapter One

On November 4, 1981 an amazing baby by the name of Tamara' Shanae' Nance was born at 9:55 a.m., by a newlywed couple of who were very happy to receive their first child. The first four years my life was excellent. My parents and I lived on the East side of Detroit in the house where my mother grew up in. I had a dog name Precious which was a Bouvier. The street that I resided on was full of love, respect, honesty and dignity. Everyone on the street was one big family. We walked in and out of each other homes as if they were our own. We all could eat dinner at home and then could go visit the neighbors for dinner as well. My family was beautiful, my mother was a fair skinned woman that stood at 5 "7". Her curves were unbelievable she was thick in the thighs and waist was small. This structure assisted her buttock that protruded from her back side. She had pretty long thick black hair that was the length of her shoulder. My father was 6 foot even, camel complexes man and his skin was flawless. He had a smile that would light up the whole room. My father parents were hard-working Americans. His father worked in the plant then retired. After his retirement he worked as a Security Guard. This was a man who had a strong passion for fishing. My fathers' mother was a nurse at a local hospital in their city. They had three sons and one daughter together. My father mother name was Evenlyn and his father name was Henry and his nick name was Banks. My mothers' family was a middle class family. My mothers' mother was a Kindergarten teacher and her father was a preacher. Their names were Mattie Ruth and Ben. They produced three beautiful daughters out of their unity. When I was growing up I saw the radiance, harmony, and love that a marriage couple brought to a family. Both grandmothers' kept me in the church every Sunday. I also went to Sunday school. With church instill in me at an early age. It made my life a lot easier. I knew that the power of pray was all a person needed to get through the bad times. Sunday dinner was the best dinner every cooked. My family appeared to have no characters flaws. I would soon find out that my perfect family wasn't so great. During this time I was the only child. I received everything I wanted for my mother, father, aunts, and grandparents. I was very, very, very spoiled. My mother would state that I wasn't spoiled I was blessed. My perfect family was missing something in my eyes and that was another child. I wanted a sister or brother to play with and to teach him or her things I knew. I had many toys. I had toys such as the Michael Jackson and MC Hammer Dolls, I whole lot of Cabbage Patch Kids and Barbie and Ken and two dolls house. All of my possession didn't make up for a little sister or brother. One Christmas I had a billion of gifts under the tree. I open all of them up and was very excited when I had received everything I wanted of course. My mother had one more surprise for me. She said, "I have one more gift", now I puzzle because I know I had open up

3

every gift in the living room. I began to look under the couches and the table thinking I missed something. She said "the gift not under there its' in my belly you have a little sister coming." That was the best gift of them all. I was the happiest little girl every. Now I have my perfect family.

Chapter two

Then when I turned five years of age I received the gift that was in my mother's belly. My aunt took me to the hospital to see my baby sister. I was so anxious. When I got to the hospital the nurse pointed out my sister to me as she laid in the incubated behind the glass with all the other babies. I asked the nurse was she sure that was my sister she assured me it was. Now I was confused because, my sister was red. She had red hair, eyebrows and skin. I thought my mother push out and alien. I had never seen a red baby before on the other hand, that was my sister I was the happy child on earth. She was so adorable I couldn't wait until my mother and new little sister came home. After a few days they came home. I and father were both excited. We both helped with all of their needs. I realized that babies don't stay babies for long because she was walking and talking in no time. We use to play hide and seek as a family. When my little sister began to walk she would hide in the strangest places such as behind the couch, dressers, and on the side of the bed. On particular day she hid behind the couch and fell asleep we couldn't find her for hours. My mother was about to call the Police. My father looked like her was going to cry. Then I decided to look behind the couch and there she was. I thought this is one weird, funny and smart red baby. I was still proud to be her big sister. This next night my sister and I was at my Aunt J home my father sister. The phone rang my aunt began to scream and holler and the top of her lungs. I woke up and went in the room to check on her to see what was going on. She was screaming something I couldn't make out what it was. As I got closer to her room I recognize what she was screaming, Pumpkin Dead! Pumpkin Dead! Pumpkin Dead was what her screams were as the echo through her townhouse. Pumpkin was her oldest brother. I t was hard for me to feel anything for my

Uncle passing because I was so young. I did feel very bad that my aunt and father had lost their oldest brother. I also thought of my favorite cousin Hank who was now fatherless. Hank was my favorite cousin because we were very close in age. On Christmas we would receive similar gift from my grandmother. Except his was in a boy style and mine is girl. We spent a lot of time together growing up. He was like a brother instead of a cousin. My uncle had three sons and one daughter that he left behind. I learned many years later that one of his sons by the name of K.D. found him dead. I don't know how true that is but that's what I was told. I could imagine what K.D. had experience at this time. The only memory I have of my uncle was he taught me how to zip my coat. This death made me acknowledge how important life was but I thought he would be here forever then all of a sudden he was gone. I couldn't fully grasp how and why. I just really felt bad for my cousin Hank who was 6 at the time. The funeral is a vague memory but I do remember the conversation me and Hank had; after the funeral Hank talk about how he didn't have a father now. I told him it was going to be alright as long we stick together. I later learned that my uncle pass from an overdose of drugs from my cousin Hank as we got older. This issue was never discussed in my family just swept under the rug. After this tragedy my family just moved on. About two weeks after the funeral I was at my fathers' parents homes in Pontiac Mi. Him and my mother was arguing in the kitchen. I couldn't believe what I was hearing. I had never heard such ruckus, commotion and confusion. I stood there in the kitchen yelling at the top of my lungs for them to stop but the just ignore me as if I didn't exist. I was so hurt and for the first time in my life tears were coming down my face. This wouldn't be the last time my face was wet. At the tender age of five I couldn't understand what the screaming and yelling was about. Then my father did the unthinkable he lifted my mother above his head and throw her down the basement steps. To add insult to injury he then grabs his friend crutch that was standing there trying to calm him down. He took the crutch to the bottom of the steps where my mother laid there helpless, sad, and hopeless. He then became to beat her with the crutch at the bottom of the step. By now my location has changed, I'm now at the top of the steps begging my father to stop beating my mother. He never did until she was black, purple and blue, like I described my mother is a fair skinned woman so every mark he put on her showed. This incident ended my perfect family..

Chapter three

By the age of six my mother and father used to go out of town a lot. They said, "They were business trips." I would often go with them to Florida, New York, Chicago, Ohio and North Carolina. I never understood what the business trips were about. I just knew I had fun, met a lot of friends and seen a lot of pretty places. On one of these trips we were in New York, I remember spending my sixth birthday in New York. We had the biggest party a kid could dream of. There were so many people, clowns, a big cake, music and I dance to my feet was sore. It was very special to have all the attention of me. It was the best birthday a child could have had. This was one business trip I enjoyed very much. My father staying on business trips he hardly every was home. Whenever my father would appear at home he would stay for two or three weeks. During this time my mother would get money from him there wasn't a limit to what we bought. I had fur coats, gold chain, and unlimited supply of shoe and clothes. All of my sister and I clothes and shoes were name brand. My father said, "His kids wore the best". Some of the time I would stay with my Aunt, Grandparents, and Neighbors. Staying with Neighbors during this time wasn't unusual because you could trust your neighbors with your children back then. One day my neighbor son was watching me my sister was with my Aunt. My neighbor had to be 18 years of age because I heard of him speak of graduating and college. I watched enough to television to figure out that 17 or 18 were the appropriate age that a person life change tremendous. Normally he would come over fix dinner and make sure I got to bed on time. Then he would stay up and watch television in our living room all night. The night was going according but then he went into the bathroom. I was watching television on the couch getting sleeping. Then he called me into the bathroom which struck me as rather odd. I went to the bathroom with him. There he stood 6 feet 3 inches towering over me I instantly became frighten. Then he pulled down his pants and pulled out his male part (penis). I have never seen anything like it I was quite amazed but still scared of course. Then he asked me to touch it, so I did because I was astonished by this big black thing. When I touch the male part it was hard. I couldn't understand why his body part was hard but it was rather interesting. Until he asked me to pull my pants down I thought WHOA now where is he going with this. I did what he said because I was unaware of what he might do to me. When I pulled down my pants he touch my private part this felt very uncomfortable. I never had anyone touch me in that area beside my mother if she was washing me up in the tub. I felt lost and confused as to why he was touching me. Then at that moment I remember what my mother had told me. She said "don't let everybody touch your private part and if they do tell me." My mother communicated with her children was efficient. I believe because she told me this she save me. I ran rapidly out the bathroom and across the street to the elderly lady house. I felt safe there and I stayed there until my mother came. My mother returned that morning; soon as I saw her face I told her what happen. My mother cried to her face was red. She was so happy I was okay. The next door neighbors never watch me again. She immediately told my father and he didn't take the information well he went next door and gave the boy a good beating. This beating I still knew was wrong but I identify with the meaning behind it. From that day forward my mother never went on any business trip with my father. She stayed at home with her children. I really appreciate her displaying such love and devotion. I always felt safe because my mother was always there. Thank GOD! My mother was always at home during the day. She would cook from us, help me with my homework and show me the proper way to clean. All her motherly duties were fulfill during the day. But at night she would disappear like a thief in the night. I knew where she was just across the street at her best friend house. I often speculate why she went over there so much in the night. My sister was still a baby she would wake up crying so I would give her a bottle my mother had the nipples and milk on the stove. I knew how to assemble a bottle because I would help my mother. I would just rock my sister back to sleep. I would guarantee her that everything was going to be okay. My mother wouldn't stay the whole night just half. It felted like the whole night when you're young and staying up with a baby. One night my mother was two-doors from our house instead of across the street. I immediately woke up out my sleep when a voice whispers to me go get your mother. I instantaneously jump out of my bed and when knock on the door really hard. I women answer the door. This woman was had dark complexion with holes up and down her arms. I told her who child I and asked her if she could please get my mother. She called my mother to the door. I told my mother to come home right now. She came with me with no problems. Then 15 minutes later we heard a big boom. We learned that morning the house that my mother was in had been cocktails or boomed. A man died from the result of this. My mother looked at me a said "you're my angle and I would never leave you at night again." From that day forward she never left the house at night again. My mother once again proved her love for her children.

14

Chapter Four

At the age of seven, my life was enticing. In attended the Detroit Public School System at this time I always got A's and B's so I stayed on the honor roll. Before I attended this school system I was in a private school. I had to wear a uniform everyday and the work was much harder. Even in private school I still maintain good grade point average. All the neighborhood children went to our neighborhood school. In the morning we would all walk to school, our school was about eight blocks from our house. My mother would get up a fix breakfast every morning a feed me and my sister. My grandmother was a teacher at another neighborhood school at this time my sister was in Pre-school. My grandmother wanted her to go to school with her. My grandmother would come get my sister every morning. While my mother and her best friend would walk me and seven children to school. I really enjoyed those time. I spend great quality time with my mother. After the school my mother would have dinner ready for us when we came home from school. She was always there to pick me up from school. My mother was very dependable as a child. This the age I discover I had an angry issue because I got into a lot of fights. There were two fights in particularly I remember. I was walking home from school one day. My mother was late picking me up so I was irritated. This girl was walking behind me talking about how I thought I was this and that. I received a lot of jealous from females coming up because I wore the best of clothing. Female often times judge me because of it. I always thought why won't they just get to know me instead of judges me or picking on me. I got tired of her talking, so I turned around a punch of in her stomach. Then I ran because I seen my mother standing at the corner. I didn't tell her what I did because I was afraid of her reaction. We lived in a tight-knit community which meant everybody knew everybody. So of course the girl's parents knew my mother. The girl's parents were in front of our house in the matter of seconds telling my mother what I did. I thought to myself my mother is going to kill me. The two main things that got us in trouble were being disrespectful to adults and we had been on your best behavior in school. My mother had a motto about school and home she said, "You must be good in school but you can act how you wanted to act home." I had a smart mouth which landed me into a lot of trouble also. I wasn't sure where punching this girl landed. Soon as the girl's mother told what I have done. My mother told that lady she didn't want to hear it and to get from in front of her house talking about her daughter. She went in the house fixed me dinner and helped me with my homework. I never got in trouble for this wrong doing.

The next altercation I got into was with another girl. I used to play outside with this once in a while. It was in the Summer time her mother used to sit on the porch and watch us play. This was a heavy set woman by the way. She was seating on the porch not wearing any underwear and legs wide open. I had

never seen anything so disgusting a day in my life.
I couldn't believe a grown woman with kids didn't
wear underwear. Then her mother went into the house.
I rolled my neck back and told her that her mamma
her nasty and trifling. Then the heffa smack me for
talking about her mother. Then I punch her in the
right cheek then the left cheek then the mouth. I ran
home because it wasn't anything left for me to do.
Next thing I know 15 girls was outside of my house.
My mother looked outside she said, "What did you
do?" I told her the whole entire story. She then told
me I had to go outside and fight. I was scare because
it was 15 girls outside. I asked her if she saw how many
girls it was. I pulled back the blinds for her and said,
"Look I'm not going out there do you see all those
girls." My mother look me eyes a said; "you are not to
be scare of nothing or nobody you only fear GOD."
Then she put a bat in my hands and told me fighting
isn't always fair. She walked me outside she told those
girls that I can fight them one on one but as soon as
they try to jump me I was going to hit them with my
bat. As she told them that I stood behind her with my
bat. All girls wasn't expected that reaction I'm sure.

They all went home. That's when I knew my mother was crazy as hell. My mother never taught me self-control or self-discipline because she didn't have any herself. This is a vital skill that every child needs to be taught.

After we would ate dinner and finish our homework. My mother made us watch all sort of movie. She made us watch the whole series of the roots. She believed that this movie was very important to African American heritage; I didn't like the movie at all because I didn't comprehend what the movie was about at first. What I did gather from the movie at a young age was Kunta Kinte and the six generations who came after him displayed unbelievable strength. The man Alex Haley who wrote this had captured our cultural heritage that ultimately spoke to all races. This movie really moved my spirit as a child.

We also watched series on an African King name ShakaZula his story was very interesting because he went through a lot in his lifetime. He was a king from the Zulu nation. The two movies made my mind think on a different level from other children. What I gather from these movies was people go through extreme measure in their lifetime but they never let it change who they are as a person.

Another T.V. we use to watch was American Most Wanted. The show was remarkable. I guess we thought we would see the bad guy one day and report him, However I like watch the show because, I like to see what crime they committed and the idea of being able to stop them. Until one day we were watching the show and you wouldn't believe who was on there it was my father, my uncle, and a friend of theirs. They were on there for attempted murder. I couldn't believe it. I was in totally devastated. The man I love with all my heart had committed a terrible crime. My father didn't appear to be this way. He was a family man who provided for his kids, wife, mother and sister. My father attended family picnics, went fishing with her father, and did shopping with her mother. I was overwhelmed with confusion. I couldn't empathize how a man with such great character how could how attempt to kill somebody. I thought how could my father be American Most Wanted, this couldn't be happening. This when I figure out that all those business trips to different states wasn't good trips. My mother just put her face in her hand and just cried. I tried to console her but all I could do was cry too. We both held each other and cried ourselves to sleep. Then that night I had a wild dream. I dream I was in the car with my father it was raining very badly. We stop at this house pulled up in the drive way. Then I heard gun shots go off. My father jump back in the car and then I heard his name go off the police scanner that he kept on the dash board. I woke abruptly very scared. I believe this dream was a bad nightmare. Then I prayed because that what both my grandmothers taught me. I was able to go back to sleep. The next day we received the Detroit News Paper; there was my father again on the front page for the crime he committed. Then I realized the dream I had the night before was true. I was in the car with my father the night he committed this vicious crime and by watching him on American Most Wanted the night before trigged the memory but it came in a dream. My father served three in half years in prison for the crime he committed. Life as I knew it would change forever because I was a daddy little girl to the tenth power. I couldn't image being without my father. How do I cope with being a fatherless child? How do I and mother manage to get by with one income coming into the family? How was my mother going to handle being a single mother with two little girls? These were the questions that were in my head when my mother told me about my father absent. I cried every night in the bathroom in my mother arms for 6 months because I missed my father. In the mist of all that crying I asked my mother what was my father occupation because I was told he did construction. I didn't believe that to be true anymore. She told me that my father sold drugs. My mother was very honest with her children I appreciated and respect her because of it. I couldn't believe her statement and I cried even harder. My mother would just hold me and say it going to be okay. Going to see him in prison clothes was torture for a child. I just wanted him home but we would have to leave him there in that inhumane place called prison. I used to think to myself this is sad for all men to be in here away from their loved one.

Chapter Five

At the age of eight my life had changed tremendously. On my eighth birthday I went to school liked normal. I was expecting a gift of some sort. I didn't really care what it was because I wasn't hard to please. When I came home my mother had a gift for me. It wasn't what I expected at all. To my surprise she had baked me cake and didn't even included icing on it because she couldn't afford to. She handed me the cake I look at her and said, "That's all." Then I notice the hurt and the pain that was in her eyes. I told her thank you. She turned away from me and just cried. I told her its okay and thanks for the effort. Then I thought to myself this is a very long way from being in New York with the clowns. How do you give a child a cake with no icing? The icing is the most important part of the cake. Now I did receive gifts from my grandparents and aunts. My mothers' gift meant the most because she was my mother. From that day forward I really didn't care about my birthday. It was just another day.

My father being absent from his family meant my mother had to get a job. My mother really didn't have to work when my father was home. My mother was introduced to my father when she was 17 years of age. His cousin Debra introduces them. Debra and my mother oldest sister Cookie had been good friends. My mother had just graduated from High School. Right out of High School. Her older sister asked her to take care of her son Ray. She kept Ray from 3 months to 5 years of age. She kept Ray because my Aunt was in school. I thought he was my brother until my Aunt came and got him one day. She went to school to be a Dentist Assistant but she didn't complete she worked in retail business at K mart but she didn't maintain that for long. She also had a job at a chocolate factory and didn't keep that either. My mother was very smart but never applied herself. She really couldn't focus on a job or herself because for years she was caught up into my father world and taking care of her family. It was very hard for her to get a job with not enough work history. Now she had to get a job to maintain the household bills and provide for her two little girls. She got on government assistant to provide for her family and stayed for years and still worked odd and in job. My grandmother was my mother backbone. We didn't go without food, clothing, and shelter. We didn't have things like we had it when my father was home. In my eyes we were poor but I was used to having so much more. My Aunt Netta moved into our house when my father left. During this time my mother got drunk almost every day and she would leave us with my Aunt Netta. Not only was I a fatherless child but I was motherless as well. My aunt was my mother baby sister. She was very fat so this was my like my mother big sister because she was huge. My Aunt Netta took very well care of us she taught me how to wash clothes and bake cakes. She would buy our 4th of July outfits and Easter and always made sure we had a good Christmas. My grandmothers and father sister was always there as well. My mother wasn't the greatest gift giver at this very significant point in a child life. Aunt Netta also talked to me a lot about everything. She was the first person to reveal to me that my mother had a drug issue. This was something I already knew it was just comforting being able to talk about it with an adult. The only catch is she was bipolar so she could go from cold to hot in the matter of second. She was supposed to take medicine for it but she told herself she didn't need to take it. I now comprehended that both my parents had a problem with drugs one was using them and the other was selling them. This made me sad from time to time because I knew how beautiful they were beside their corrupted lifestyle they live. I knew to grow up and be much better than them. In my eyes my parents wasn't bad people they had just choose the wrong path in life. I wasn't going to let their path determine my future. I value my life much more than my parents did. At this age I wanted to be a lawyer so I read many books. My grandmothers used to tell me that reading was fundamental.

One day I was playing outside then my mother called me and my sister in to introduce us to someone.

She sat us on the couch a little boy came into our living room. Then my mother spoke and said, "This is your brother." He was a peculiar looking little boy. His skin was darker than our and his facial feature were way different. I was baffled because, I didn't know I had another sibling but my heart was filled with joy because I had a brother. A man walk in behind him and this was his father who my brother looked exactly alike. That explained why he didn't look like me, my sister, or my mother. At this point in my life I knew of my father was the only man my mother had ever been with. I asked where this boy and his daddy come from. She explained that her and my father broke up when I was 3 years old. Then she came across Fred during this break up and they produce a child together. Her and my father eventually got back together. When they got back together he found out about this situation. That's what he and my mother were arguing about that night in his mother's home. My father take on the whole situation was that my mother had betrayed him even though they were broke up she wasn't suppose to go to another man. So he lost his mind and beat her. On that day Fred and my brother (Peewee) moved into our home. Living with Peewee and Fred was horrible. Now Peewee had a grudge against my mother because he felt abandoned by her. I also felt the same way because she uses to leave me for the streets. We tried to kill her. My mother favorite cook aide was grape. She told us to make her some. So we went in the kitchen got the entire ingredient together. After we were finish putting the sugar, Kool-Aid, and water together. My brother said, "Let's put choral lighter fluid in there. My mother bar be que a lot so we knew exactly where to go get it. Her room was located up stair, so we ran up stair and gave it to her. We stood at the bottom of the steps waiting to see what was going to happen. Then she dash down those stairs as if she had wings on her back. Then next thing I know I felt the most excruciating pain I had ever felt in my life. The pain went from my head to toes all at once. Then I apprehended that she was hitting me and my little brother with a thick orange stitching cord. She hit us again. I fell to the floor and told her my name was "Toby" this threw off her train of thought off her immediately stop. I felt like she was the master and I was Kunta Kinte. That pain was

28

unbearable. She said, "Both of you are to respect me no matter what I do because I am your mother you're suppose to honor your mother and father." I was so happy she stops hitting me I didn't know what to do. Once she stops hitting us I asked her how she knew. She explained that she smell the fluid once she put the cup up to her lips. I never tried to kill my mother again. I just got smart with her a lot because I really didn't respect her. I believe she didn't respect herself. I saw the back of her hand on many occasions for my smart mouth. She beat me with a shoe and the iron cord on two different occasions all for my smart mouth. My little brother was a hand full also. He sat our basement on fire, fought constantly at school and on the street we lived on. He used to steal money that he found around the house. She would beat us with whatever she could put her hands on. I told her it was child abuse her response to that was living in the system is worst than here so take your pick. If you would keep your mouth close you wouldn't get hit. If your brother would stop doing crazy stuff he wouldn't get hit. In the mist of us getting beat she was getting beat by Fred. My house was total in kaucus. Fred would back hand my mother from the same reason she use to hit me in my mouth. My mother would stomp all over that man ego, she was the queen at verbal abuse. He really didn't appreciate it. The bottom of her lip stayed swollen. After he would hit her she would still run her mouth. That's when the black eyes started. Fred needed a way to control my mother. She wouldn't shut up no matter how hard he hit her. When he would hit her I would find her somewhere in the house and put a cold towel on her face to try to keep down the swelling in her face. It was hard to see her face black and blue and then the next day she wore sunglass. I knew my mother was strong woman I couldn't believe she was going through this. It really hurt to see my mother get abuse like this. What puzzle me the most is why she wouldn't put him out of her house? My father had already beaten her so why was she taking this from another man. She didn't learn from the first man who put his hands on her. I asked her why she was taking it and she said "your grandfather was the first to black my eye when I was 7 year old, then your daddy, and now Fred; abuse is a learn behavior you just get use to it." I didn't understand how you get use to somebody using your face as a punching bag. I never wanted to learn this behavior. I wanted a man who treated me like a queen.

One day we were playing outside as usually. My mother ran out the house like she was getting chase by a dog but it's wasn't a dog it was Fred. In his hand he was a silver solid bat. Fred beat my mother all up and down the street with that bat. The entire neighborhood watched as if they were watching breaking news on 2, 4, and 7. I stood there in pain as I watch him hit her. I didn't know what to do. My mother screams were so loud it echo the whole street. Each time she screamed I screamed inside. I felt vulnerable. For the first time I didn't cry by this time in my life I was amuse to pain. The only person who came to her rescue was her best friend. She came out her house with a knife and told him if he didn't put that bat down she was going to stab him dead. He put the bat down and she took my mother in her house and nursed her wounds. I went in the house to check on her. I still didn't cry or feel anything. The look in my mother eyes was dark and lifeless. She was black, blue, purple, and red from head to toe. The ambulance showed up shortly after. She didn't return home for a couple days. We stayed with my grandmother while she was in the hospital. By the grace of God she didn't have any broken bones. They kept her for a couple of days so she could build her strength back up. When my mother returned home I asked why he did that. She said, "Because she spoke to a man she had being knowing since grade school so Fred felt intimated and insecure" My mother once told me that everyone has a story. I was curious to know what Fred story was. I asked my mother what made him so vicious at time. She said, "His mother used to beat the hell out of him so he didn't know how to express himself correctly." In my eyes Fred wasn't that bad of a man he just had an angry problem. He took good care of me and my sibling. She never told the police and Fred still live in our house after that event. My heart turned real cold I want to kill him in his sleep. I couldn't believe a person could be so cold to beat somebody with a bat. On the other hand a person could be so stupid to let them beat them with a bat. This incident displayed my mother weakness and I believe I gain a lot of strength for her weakness.

Chapter Six

At the age of nine my insight on life was delusional. I was very confused, lost, and unhappy. I often times thought about killing myself. When that thought ran across my head I thought about my little sister and brother. I didn't want to leave them in the cold world in this disrupted family by themselves. I live for them but deep down I just wanted to die. Thank God I was blessed to know that I had a friend in Jesus. I knew this because I stayed in church every Sunday. I knew that all of my life experiences were supposed to make me stronger. I knew that the lord won't put me through no more on you than you can bear. I was just confused as to why I went through so much a young age. I also knew not to question God. Later on in that year my father was released from prison. I was the happy little girl every. He came home and mother was still with Fred. They didn't get back together. I really want them to. He moved in with his girlfriend at the time that lived in Lansing Mi. I and my sister went to live with him because I was fed up with living in Fred's drama. My father girlfriend lived with her mother. We called her grandma. Now grandma was a real hilarious lady. That loved her grandchildren. She made life a joy because she was so honest. She kept all of us on our P's and Q's. Her favorite meal to cook was beans and cornbread. Grandma explained that we were all family. She never made us feel unwanted. Living in Lansing wasn't pleasing either. The reason being the house was stayed in was very big. It was people everywhere like it was an army base. The first night we went there we slept on a cot, which was very comfortable. I never seen so many people in my life situated in one house. With all these people in this house my father introduced my sister and I to a little girl. He told us this little girl was our sister. This blew my mind because this little girl was the same size as the sister I already had. I found out my sister in Lansing was 2 weeks younger than my little red sister. Now I had an extra brother my mother and an extra sister by my father. I thought to myself this is a mess. I was still happy and embrace her. Both of my sisters didn't get along for a while. They fought almost every day. I used to tell them to stop but they felt they must defend each of their territory. They both were used to being the baby now they had to share this title. One day they locked themselves in the room and we tried to get them out of there. All we could her was rumbling and tumbling. They finally unlock the door and came out and said "We aren't going to fight no more." This was funny because they made peace with one another in their own way. They were only 4 years old. In this whole house full of people the person I attached to the most was my cousin Myrun. He was close to my age; I was 3 weeks older than him. Myrun was so sweet, funny, and positive. He made you feel like a warm cookie inside. This was another favorite cousin beside Hank. While I was in Lansing I and Myrun held deep childhood conversations just like me and Hank. For instance, I told him one day I enjoyed being there with him and his family. I really missed my mother he reassured me that my mother was okay and I was going to be okay also. I really believe his words. My father took us to see my mother almost every weekend. On one weekend were on our way to see her. But my father got a phone call that his mother was dead. We went Beaumont Hospital instead of Detroit. They wouldn't let me see my grandmother. I stayed in the waiting room with a friend of the family. When this death occurred I was very sad. I had a lot of great time with my grandmother. We used to watch Wheel of Fortune, Jeopardy and Perry Mason together. I learned how to cook chicken and dumpling from her. Most important on Sunday she kept me in church. I was in church for Sunday school, Morning Service, and Afternoon Service. We stayed in church from 7:00 a.m. to 8:00p.m. Don't let the church have a concert we didn't get out of church to the next day it seemed like. I was so exhausted from church I didn't know what to do. She kept me and my sister dressed well when it was time to go to church. We had on cashmere coats, dresses that flurried out at the bottom, our hats, our dresses, and socks all matched. I felt like a princess. I believe at that time the only thing I liked about church was getting dress for church. My Grandma Evenlyn cooking was awesome. These were the memories I had of my grandmother as I waited for my father to return to the waiting room. For the first time in the long time I cried like a new born baby. I was so hurt that my grandmother was gone. Even though I couldn't stand church at the time I thanked my grandmother for introducing me to the spirit of the Lord. I was able to handle her death better because I knew how to pray. My grandmother Evenlyn taught me the power of prayer. I prayed with my grandmother day in and day out. I dropped to my knees in that waiting room and prayed for healing and asked God to help my family with their grief. She told me to say in Jesus name after yours prayer so I did. Although I was very sad by me knowing the ability to pray I felt a little better when I got off my knees. I then knew why I stayed in church so much. My grandmother was putting a seed in me that I was going to need for the rest of my life. I now thank my Grandmother for allowing me to know the Lord and his son Jesus. Later on that day I asked my Aunt J how did my grandmother pass she said, "complication of Lupus; My Aunt J had Lupus and one of my Grandmother Sister pass from Lupus also. This disease is hereditary and runs in our family. I looked up lupus because J wanted to know in case J got it one day. This disease weaken your immune system attacks healthy cells and tissues by mistake. This can ultimately damage your joints, skin, blood vessels and organs.

Now at the funeral J sat by my father and his girlfriend. J looked up at that moment J notice something about my father girlfriend. She was a dark complexion woman, her skin was rough, she had holes in her face like pot holes, and his lips protruded and spread out across her face. She was the completed opposite of my mother and question why is my father this nice looking man sitting next to her. Two rows up a head of us there was my mother is a gray dress that showed her wonderful shape body. Her face was clear no cut, bruise, or black eye. She was beautiful. J took my sister and sat by my mother. J was so happy to see her. J cried. Then notice my sister crying because J grandmother was gone and reality sunk in J was at a funeral not a reunite. Then my tears of happiness turned to tears of sadness. My poor Aunt J at her mother's funeral she screamed and hollered for a long time. She was holding the casket screaming momma don't leave me! I look back at my father and he had one tear dropping from his face. I figure he was in so much pain that's all his body could generate was one tear. My mother took the death hard also. She cried a lot. As I looked around at all my cousins and grandmother's sister and the entire church member who were her friends; it wasn't a dry eye in the church and the church was filled with people from the top to the bottom. Some of the people didn't even have a seat they stood and cried. I knew that my Grandmother made a positive impact on others just as well as myself and her family.

After the funeral my mother told me she had finally left Fred that day. She also made him take Peewee because she couldn't tolerate his behavior. The reason she left Fred, he didn't want her to come to my Grandmother funeral. He pulled out a gun and pistol whip her somehow she got away from him beating her with the gun. My mother had amazing strength she always fought back rather it was with her mouth or fist. To try and regain control he shot at her as she ran up the street. She explained she ran to her zigzag up the street because bullets shoot straight. She said, "She was coming no matter what because Evenlyn was like her mother.

My father also had something to reveal after the funeral also. He took me and my sister into the basement of our Pontiac home where he grew up in. Which were also the same steps he threw my mother down? Every time I walked those steps I have that painful memory. There was a cute little chocolate boy down there he said, "This is your brother Quan. The first time I saw him I thought he is so cute. We ran and gave him a hug. Then we all played together in that basement for the rest of the night. Quan and my brother Peewee are a year apart and my brother. Quan is older. While he was beating my mother for her child because he felt betrayed. He already had a child that we didn't know about. That's crazy. I wanted somebody to come beat the hell out of my father because now he had two children to my mother one child. That was okay because he was the man. I understood the different between what a man could do and a woman couldn't. I thought it wasn't fair there needed to be some type of balance between the men and women. As I went to sleep that night after the funeral I reflected on my mother and father life. I thought my mother must have superpower or nine lives like a cat because; she have now been pistol whipped, shoot at, beat with a solid steel sliver bat, threw down a flight of stairs, had 3 kids, on drugs, drink liquid, some many black eyes you lose count and she still here. This woman should be dead by now but she's still standing. She has strength that's unheard of or unseen. If I wasn't a witness to the majority of the beaten I would have thought a person was lying if they had told me. I thought God is saving her live for something, I didn't know what it was. I was just happy to still have a mother. I surprise at my father life also. He had just got out of prison for attempted murder. He stayed skipped from state to state like he was playing hop scotch. He had 4 kids. He was still here also. He got to attend his mother funeral like he was a normal citizen. I was happy to have both of my parents no matter what lifestyle they lived. One thing I commend my mother and father for was never exposed their children to their life styles. I never saw drugs or my mother high. They managed to make me believe that they were normal. They took care of their children the best way they knew how. We returned back to Lansing to finish the school year. I wouldn't leave Lansing without and story to tell of course. When we first got to Lansing I notice my sister had a bite mark on her chest. I asked her how did it get there she said, "Her mother bit her." I thought Wow, how extreme is that? My father girlfriend tried to eat me and my sisters two days after I asked my sister that question. Yes I said, "Eat". One night me and my sisters and sister brother was in the living room talking and laughing with Grandma. M y sister mother came into the door unexpected as if she was a wild animal. She was breathing real hard and making a usual noise. She was growling like a bear ready for attack. My sister brother immediately picked her up and took her staight across the street to the neighbor house. He put in her arm like he was cuffing a football. He ran so fast to safety. I thought he had fire on his feet. At the twinkled of an eye my Grandma got in front of me and my red sister. I was scared for my life. We were crying so hard my face went numb. I knew that Grandma was going to protect us. I had never seen a human being at like an animal. One of the cousins came and pushed her out the house and put her in the car. When it was over my whole body was without sensation I was in complete shock. From this day forward I thought of her as being a monster. I couldn't sleep and my father wasn't there. He returned that morning. I asked him if he would please take me and my sister out of that home. We left that morning.

Chapter Seven

At the age of ten we left Lansing but not to return
home to my mother to live but with my Aunt J. I
really wanted to go home. My father was convinced
that my mother was unfit to take care of her kids
because she had an issue with drugs. I didn't care what
issue she had I wanted to be with her not bouncing
form pillow to post. We had to stay with someone
who he felt was safe with because of his ego. He
would still take us to see her on the weekend but that
wasn't enough. She still remained in the same house
everything worked just fine and she was still loving
and caring. I wanted to stay with her or my father but,
we couldn't stay with him because he was unstable. To

top it all off my Aunt was mean. Despite how mean she was it was way better than being in Lansing. She provided for us and did all the necessary things a caretaker is suppose to do. Her attitude, behavior, demeanor was very negative. Nothing could please this woman. It was her way or the highway. This was very uncomfortable living arrangement. She made you feel like she didn't love you. She had no compassion. I often times would wonder why was she so mean. I thought it was because she had Lupus and she had lost her mother and brother. She worked with abused and neglected children. I thought her job affected the way she ran her household. I realize that she still had no business being so mean. It wasn't just towards kids it was everybody. She was very strict. So had so many rules and regulations she couldn't have been the president. I couldn't even hold a decent conversation with her. My mother was the complete opposite I could talk to her about everything. At this age I shut down and stop talking. I believe all the life had been sucked out of my body. Being in this woman household I grew to be insensitive. Once was a happy little girl now I became dull? Only time I had life is when I was around my mother and the street I grew up on. The weekends I would go see her I felt relief. I got to talk to her and express myself. I asked her why my father girlfriend had such bizarre behavior that night. She said, "Drugs have a different reaction with different people." I asked her why my Aunt was so mean, she said "She wasn't sure but she's a Virgo and her father was a Virgo and that acted the same way they liked to be in control so pray for her." My mother was a Virgo she acted nothing like that. My mother was crazy but she wasn't mean. Although my Aunt I was mean. I appreciated her behavior after all. She instills discipline, structure, balance, and boundaries that I needed. She also implemented self-control, self-discipline within me and this is something I need a great deal. These skills helped me later on in life. I didn't learn these traits from my mother. While we were in my Aunts' household my mother and father was trying to mend their relationship. At the end of this year they got back to together. It didn't last for long. By the end of that summer they were broke up again. My mother said because my father yet again through down some flight of stairs. I wasn't there to witness this catastrophe, Thank the Lord! After this my mother was fed up of getting beat on so she left him. I and my sister went along for the ride as usual. In the last of the Summer Days, I thought I was just going to run up and down the street and play like always. My mother had another idea. This time she was leaving my father she really meant it. We went back to our home on the Eastside for about a week. Then she came to me and my sister and said, "We must go somewhere where your father can't find us." At this age I began to cuss in my head which I learned this from my mother. She had a potting mouth. When she spoke these words in my head I said "Where in the hell am I going now." That day we packed up as much clothes as we could take. Then my Grandmother dropped me and mother and sister off at this big brown building. The building looked scary. When went into the building and a lady greeted us and welcome. I still wondering, what the hell in going on and what is she welcoming us in to? We sat in her office. She told us the rules to this place. Some of the rules were me and my sister had to be sleep at a certain time. If we left this place we had to be in by a certain time. We had a bedtime, curfew, and meal time was served at specific time also. Then she walks us down a hall way to our resting area. As I walk the hall way. I felt like it was my last and finally walk. She opened up the door to our room. The room had a one bunk bed and one closet. Now our house on the Eastside of Detroit had three bedrooms and a basement, living room and kitchen. I thought how we are supposed to stay in such a small area. I understood she wanted to get away from my father but, how was coming to this place going to help that circumstances. I asked my mother what was this place she said, "This is a shelter for batter women, they are going to help us get away from your father and we won't be here long." I really didn't want to be here I felt homeless. I made light of the situation like I always did I remain strong because if I didn't my mother would cry. I hated to see her cry. As the oldest child it's a lot of pressure put on my shoulder. The end of the summer wasn't that bad in the shelter. Everyday my mother took us out and we would go to the movie or go Downtown Detroit to the Festivals. We would look for different houses to live in everyday too. The shelter only gave the women

30 days to stay there. I really saw that my mother was strong and had ambition. I haven't seen her like this in years. Another positive point was my mother received counseling to fight her childhood demons. I receive counseling as well. This was good to talk to someone beside my mother because I could totally express myself. Our 30 days was reaching its peak. Since we couldn't find a house in Michigan within the allotted time the shelter provided. The shelter was going to pay for us to go out of state. We just had to pick the state. My mother put all the name of the 50 states in a hat. My little sister receives the opportunity to pull the name out of the hat because she was the baby. She pulled out the state Georgia. So we got on the Greyhound bus and went to Atlanta. The bus ride was long and tiresome. Riding a bus was exciting because I never been on one before. When we finally arrived in Atlanta this state was magnificent. The entire tree were big and had peaches on them. The city was clean and pretty. When we got there we had to stay in another shelter again to my mother found us a place to stay? We only stayed in this shelter for 1

week. She didn't want us to go to school from a shelter. She quickly found us an apartment.

Chapter Eight

At the age eleven I was in Atlanta starting middle school. During these school years I learned a lot. There public school system was very different. I learned how to note taking, developed a positive attitude, the material the school system was teaching was far in advance of what I learned in Detroit Public School. One teacher explained that the school system in the south was much tougher in the North because the south was oppressed for many years. They really wanted their children to learn so they really value education. It was like I was taking college courses. This school was very challenging. I was on the honor roll the whole year. The teachers were very passionate about teaching. Since the teachers were so passionate about the subject they were teaching I really want to learn. I came out of my shell and became a social butterfly. I had a lot of friends. I hung around 5 or 6 girls in meticulous. We use to get in trouble a lot in class for talking and playing. The apartment we stayed in was very spacious. This was my first time staying in an apartment it most definitely beat those shelters. My mother was great during this time. She found a job and worked every day. She also went to a treatment center daily to get off drugs. She got home around 6:00 p.m. every day. My little sister would stay after school for latch key. It was my responsibility to go get her before 5:00 p.m. First for the time in years I had a happy home life and school. Being in the south was a beautiful experience in my life. Atlanta was filled with many friendly people who showed us the ends and out of Atlanta. My mother has always been a social butterfly so she made friend easily. Every holiday we spent down there was beautiful. For the first time in a long time my mother bought us gift. On holiday like Thanksgiving or Christmas we would go over her friend's house to eat. They knew we didn't have any family there so they welcome us into their home. We went to her friend Betty house that she met at work for Thanksgiving. Betty was a short little petty lady and had a husband name Al with a big belly. When we walked into the house the aroma for the kitchen smelled good. I couldn't wait to eat. As we sat down at the big long brown wood table my mother and Betty was placing the food on the table. I just wanted to eat everything on there. We all held hands and prayed and blessed the food. My mother made me and my sister plates. There was macaroni and cheese, dressing, turkey, sweet potatoes, greens, and potatoes salad. I couldn't wait to indulge in this good food. I eat one thing at a time. My mother told me I get my eating style from my Uncle Pumpkin. I started eating my macaroni and cheese that's my favorite dish. My mother once said, "everything glitter and gold." I knew what that meant because that macaroni and cheese looked cheesy, rich and thick. When I bit down on it the noodles were hard. I was very disappointed. I moved on to the next dish the greens. I was scare to eat those because the color of the greens was turquoise. I knew greens weren't to suppose to be that color. The sweet potato wasn't sweet enough, the turkey was dry and the potatoes salad the potatoes wasn't cooked all the way. Each item I bit into was horrific. I thought this is a joke the real food is about to come out the kitchen. It wasn't no joke this lady seriously prepared this dinner. I looked up at my mother with a disgusted look on my face. She knew exactly what the look was for. She just gave me a kindred smile. That smile meant I feel your pain but please don't say anything. She know I am very out spoken I was about to go off right there at that dinner table. Then Betty had the nerve to ask how the food is. My mother looked at me again. I really wanted to tell that lady that her food was nasty and she should be ashamed of herself to produce a meal this dreadful. I wanted to reach across the table a smack her. I couldn't have done a better job than this. My mother started cooking when she was nine. When I reached nine she taught me how to cook too. My mother looked at Betty and responded to her question by saying it's good. For the first time in history my mother told a lie to prevent for hurting the lady feeling. Well at this point I was mad, hungry and ready to go home. We didn't leave right then the adults had small talk over the plate full of garbage. Then Betty and my mother cleared the table and washed the dishes. Betty was the one to pick up my plate she noticed that I took little bites out of her food. She said, "what wrong baby you wasn't that hungry." I looked up to her and responded no not much. In reality I was so hungry I could eat two cows. We put our jackets on and Al drove us home and invited us to Christmas dinner. I wanted to tell him I not coming near your wife food on no day. We got home my mother laughed she thought the whole thing was amusing. I didn't find anything funny. We talked about Betty's food for about 4 weeks after that. Lucky my mother had prepared Thanksgiving dinner for us at home. I got to eat normal good tasting food. To this day I don't eat any one cooking I don't know. I don't like the element of surprise. We didn't visit any more friends for dinner. My mother befriended this lady who lived in our apartment building name Imani she was a Muslim. Imani had three big headed boys. Two of her sons were about 5 or 6 years old. She had one son name Abdul he was two years older than me. My mother friendship with Imani was beautiful. Imani was very positive, always gave great advice, she was a very peaceful lady. It was a joy to be around Imani. We use to spend a lot of time with her. I believe I picked up on some of her peaceful ways. She never cussed or raise her voice for nothing, Even if her children were getting on her nerves. This is something my mother did frequently. One evening she took my mother to see Louis Farkkan he came to speak in Atlanta that year. My mother came back with the most fascinating look in her eyes. She spoke of Louis in such great dimension. She told me he was an extraordinary man. She learned a lot from his speech. My mother was a changed woman after she saw him she became more peaceful. She lived her life in Atlanta with grace and elegant. I believe Louis made her think about her corrupted lifestyle. She just made a drastic change. I was very proud of her no found determination to change. Christmas in Atlanta was one of the most memorable. My mother, sister and I had put up and decorated this Christmas tree together. It was very big. On Christmas day is wasn't no snow which was strange to me because I used to being in Michigan. Under the trees they were a ton of present for me and my sister. We had so many presents I could believe my eyes. On this Christmas day my mother made up for the times she didn't get us that many presents. What made it so special is that she did it all by herself, with no help from her mother, my father, and her sisters. She proved to me how astonishing she was. The only piece missing from under the Christmas tree was a new television set. In our apartment we had a little 13 inch T.V. I wanted a big one. The next day we went looking for T.V. We were out all day looking for a T.V. that was just the right size. At that time we didn't have a car. Matter of fact we never had a car but whenever we needed to go someone my Grandmother was always available. The day grew to night as we look for this T.V. When we finally found one it was last and Atlanta didn't properly have transportation such as buses, cabs, accessible like Detroit at this time. The T.V. my mother found was 27 inch she carry that television set up 13 blocks with two kids late at night. When we got home I knew my mother had superpower because she carried that size T.V. for that long was mind-boggling. We set the T.V. in our living room and watched it that night on the couch. We were watching 20/20 on there was a girl was talking about being molested by her cousin. I felt so bad for the girl. I had experience being violated myself. Then my mother explained to us if anybody touches you in your private area tell me. My little sister exposed with tears. We asked with great concern, what wrong what wrong, she said, K.D. touched me! K.D. touched me! We weren't prepared for that my mouth swung open and I was speechless. She wasn't done she said my sister brother in Lansing had sex with her in her butt. My mother was pissed. If we had been in Michigan at the time I do believe she would have killed both of them. I just went to my room and cried. I was filled with angry and guilt. I thought it was my fault I was my sister protector. How could I let something like this happen to her? Where was I when this was going on? I failed as a big sister. I asked for her to come her then I didn't protect her. When my sister told us it trigged a vague memory of K.D. touching me too. I can't remember all of it. I was hurt and in pain cause I felt my sister pain. My sister news send me into total shock. I couldn't believe she carried this burden at such a young age. I wanted to take the pain from her. How could my cousin and brother take advantage of a baby? She was 6 years old when were in Atlanta. I began to do the timeline. She was 3 when we lived with my Aunt J so my cousin touched her at the age of 3. That was sick and sad. When were in Lansing she was 5 years old my sister brother when inside of her butt at 5 now that even sicker. I began ill and threw up all my dinner that night. Then I had a seizure that night. It was stress induce. My grandfather had seizure so I inherit them from him. I started having seizure at the age of 3. They would skip through the years. I wouldn't have them all the time. This seizure was the first in about 4 or 5 years. I was off my seizure medicine because we thought they were gone. My mother had to take me to the hospital that night. They put me back on my seizure medicine. My new found love for life was gone my mother was also. I told my sister I was going to help her get through it. I talk to her all the time about her feeling after that. From the day forward I watched her like a hawk. My sister and I grew very close at this point in our life we realized all we had were each other. We left Atlanta at the end of the year because my mother was home sick. I really wanted to stay. We went along for the ride once again. We took the long bus ride back to Michigan. My Aunt J picked us up from the bus stop. She took us to our home in Detroit. I wasn't happy to be home at all. I really enjoyed my life with me, my mother and sister in Atlanta. I had a lot of unanswered question such as; would my mother go back to her old ways? Would her and my father get back together? And most important, how was my sister going to cope with this childhood trauma? When we returned to our home my Aunt Netta was there. She handed my mother a stack of mail. In the stack of mail was a letter from the State of Michigan. The letter stated that they tried to contact her on many occasions but the results were negative. The letter further stated that her son had became ward of the state he would be able to contact us when he was 18 years of age. For now she had no rights to her son. She called Fred asked him what was going on. Fred stated that Peewee pushed a girl down some steps at school. He beat him and Peewee ran away. The police picked PeeWee up walking around Belle Isle he had bruises all on his face, chest, back, and legs and they determinate his rights as a father. The police went to our house on many occasions but my Bipolar Aunt never told my mother while we were in Atlanta. My mother called my Aunt Netta everything but the child of GOD. She cried and said "she would have came back and got her son if she knew." I knew this was going to send my mother over the edge because her son had been taken away and her daughter was molested. My father was out of town when we got back of course. The day after we got back my mother confronted my Aunt J about my cousin touching my sister. She didn't believe her. But her boyfriend at the time believe my mother. Still to this day my Aunt J doesn't believe it happen. It doesn't matter. We never got a chance to see my father when we returned from Atlanta. He got caught with abundance of drugs and they gave him a 10 years sentence, which he served 7. I read the police report to see what happen. It stated that my father was sleep in the car in Ohio. He was with her girlfriend (the monster) from Lansing. She was wandering the road looking for drugs. The police picked her up and she basically took them back to the car where my father was. My father tried to hide but they still caught him. Now I felt not only was she a monster but stupid too. She was a person that didn't need to do drugs. She was a nice, sweet lady with a big heart.

Chapter Nine

While I was twelve and thirteen I lived back with my Aunt J. The question I raised about my mother came true. She wasn't strong enough to deal with my father being gone, her son gone and her daughter violated. My mother was so deep into drugs it was ridiculous. I realize that being on drugs is a disease. She had become a person I really didn't know. I barely saw her anymore. She would come get us on the weekend for time to time. My grandmother Ruth was my source and rock during these times. She talked to me all the time about the family. How I was supposed to be independent. But I was still depressed for these two years. It really hurt me to my soul to not having a father. These were my teenage years I really needed him. I just became a walking zombie. I didn't feel anything. My heart turned bitter and cold. I didn't have feeling anymore and didn't care about anybody else feel either. I think I ate everything but the refrigerator. They would say I was big boned like my Aunt Netta. I was simply chunky and fat. I used food as my comfort. I went to school in the Pontiac School System coming from Atlanta school system it was such a big different. I didn't like anybody in that school or city. My life was terrible, my mother gone, my father gone and I was struck in the mean lady house (Aunt J) where she treated kids like shit but spoiled them at the same time. My sister left and lived with my mother back in Detroit. My sister didn't like my Aunt behavior. This was the first time in history being separated for my lil red baby I was crushed. I just wanted to crawl under a rock wishing everything would go away. I became very quite I tried to kept a smile on my face. I had friends because I stayed in and out of Pontiac school system. I really didn't like any of them they were all fake and weird. My friends in Detroit and Atlanta were more realistic and different. They accepted people for who they were. It was a lot of clique and people judging your every move. These people in the clique would fall out with each other. They didn't even know the true beauty of friendship. I just wanted to punch these kids in the face. These kids just didn't know what real life was. The boys weren't like that. I got along with them, mainly because I lived in Aunt J house with all boys. Which were my cousins Hank, K.D. and my brother Quan stayed right around the corner from us? I understood boys better than females. One female I became friends with and that was it. She was cool and fit my personality. Her mother was a Virgo but the Virgo like my mother; the one that talked to her kids but crazy not controlling and mean. I used to sit and talk to her mother for hours. This gave me an outlet because I didn't talk to my Aunt and couldn't talk to my mother. My Aunt Tammy was somebody I could talk to also. My Tammy used to be my Uncle's childhood girlfriend. After they broke up she never left the family. She kept me grounded because she was a Scorpio like me so she knew exactly how I was. I could tell him anything, and she kept my hair done because she was a hairstylist. She would buy me and my sister school clothes all the times. These two years for me were very sad. I was fatherless for real this time. My cousin and I, Hank talked about this issue. He would say. One day you will see your father, I never will. I told him; although you can't see your father he lies within his heart. Even though I would see my father one day I needed him now. Then Hank looked at me and said, "I am your father now." I laughed at him when he spoke those words. He was serious; Hank didn't let me do anything. Boys weren't an option. He said books first. He would scare all the boys a way. I was scared of him like he was my real daddy. I wouldn't do anything because Pontiac is so small you could spit over it. I didn't want any information getting back to my cousin. So I just didn't do anything with any boys. The four people who got me through these years were my sweet dear grandmother, my cousin Hank, my friend mother and my Aunt Tammy. My grandfather (Banks) passed away during this years. He passed from Cancer located in pancreatitis. Now my Grandfather spoke his mind and loved to fish. He would carry a lot of change in his pockets.

When he would go to sleep I would take it and go to the ice-cream truck. The Hospice lady used to come to our house and check on him, she often asked my Grandfather was he ready to die he said, "Yeah." I watched my Grandfather slowly slip away but it wasn't sad because he was a strong man. He passed with peace and love in his heart. His funeral was held at the same church as my grandmother Evenlyn. My father wasn't able to attend this funeral like a normal citizen. The prison brought him to the funeral before everyone arrived. He was wearing handcuff and chain on his feet. I was very hurt because I had lost both of my Grandparents on my father side. I was very close with them. I knew had one set of grandparents still alive.

Chapter Ten

At the age of 14 my life became easy. Thoughts and feeling entering high school as enter the last stretch of schooling. I was more than ready to then ready to enter the world and get from the strongholds of everybody self-destruction I was surrounded by. I was very exciting about entering high school mainly because I couldn't wait to be on my own because I personally was looking forward to be in another world beside the world in my surrounding. For example, my mother world was dark and lonely her life decision to cure her miserable state of mind was drugs and chasing men that aren't any good to her. It was all so sad. When I became 14 years of age I started to analysis my surrounding and I asked more questions. In the process of doing this I discover my mother's self-destruction in her own adulthood came from a very trouble childhood. She didn't have the mind capabilities to erase her troubling childhood. When I looked at my mother in a deeper tone I realize she only was looking to be loved by someone or something. Whether it was drugs or men she needed something to depend on to cure the little girls that was screaming out for help as a child. My grandfather's abuse was just the tip of the iceberg. My grandmother's nice, sweet, and timid behavior also affected her. My grandmother took my grandfather's abuse for years more mentally than physical. She never stood up to my grandfather's when it came to herself or her kids. It has been stated that my grandfather molested my mother's other two sister. My grandmother was introduce with the information but never did anything about it. This was a horrible event to my mother as child because she had to watch her two sisters endure pain and it was nothing she could do about it. By grandmother never standing up to my grandfather's my mother couldn't acquire any communication skills or a sense of balance from this. She just learned how to take the back seat and enjoy the ride just like my grandmother did, Although my grandfather was a good family man as far as keeping his children in church. He took them on family trip to the south every summer. He was a great provider when it came to keeping up the household. My mother's and sister wore the best of clothes and shoes. Always had food and they never worried about shut off notices? He planted a great seed within them. He installed great morals and values. On the negative side he was a control freak. He controls every aspect of his family lives. As a child my mother could only ride her bike in the driveway not up and doesn't the street like the other children. They really couldn't go in any parties, basketball or football games unless my grandmother went with them. If they would try to seek, my grandfather would show up where ever they were and embarrass the hell out of them. So my mother never had freedom as child, on top of being abused, and she didn't learn how to maintain a backbone either because she wasn't taught. My mother was a beautiful woman on the inside and out. Her spirit was warm and comforting. As I took all of these facts into account I really felt sorry for my mother.

When I look into my father's life into perspective I realize that he was basically spoiled rotten. My grandmother gave him whatever he wanted. I believe this totally alter his life. She never told him no and stayed by his side whether he was wrong or right. I believe that when he made a conscious decision to deal marijuana at the age of 14 somebody could have stopped him. Then again my grandmother was only being a mother she probably didn't realize that her child would become a career criminal. My father was also a womanizer which he got from her father. His behavior was also learned. My father didn't have the mind state to stop his self-destruction because of money. He also had an addiction just as my mother. He was addicted to the idea of fast money. He had the ability to do whether he wanted when he wanted because he had the money. He also grew up in church, went fishing, and family trip. His family structure was wonderful. My father had a magnificent personality; he was so laid back and beautiful communication skills. He couldn't have been anything he wanted because he had charm and charisma which are rare commodities among some human. Despite his God giving talent he choose the life of the streets which landed him to serve a 10 years sentence, how sad.

Often times during this year I would sit and ponder about my brother Peewee. I wonder was he getting treated right in the system. I knew that children who were placed in the system life ended up being worst then the life they left because the foster parents wouldn't treat the child accurately. I worried that he wasn't being treated how he shouldn't been treated. I knew my brother had a zero policy for nonsense so I knew he was somewhere driving somebody crazy. I really missed my brother Peewee. I hope and prayed we re-unite one day. I felt lost without my sibling. The separation and suspends about his well being wasn't good for my mental state. Nevertheless I knew he was a survivor and whatever he was he was doing well. I just knew he had the will power to succeed just like me. I took comfort knowing my brother characteristic. I remember one time we didn't have no food and me and my brother ate a syrup sandwich. I have to say that was the best syrup sandwich ever.

When I look at my life now at 14 years of age I deem that my life story wasn't going to be a tragedy but a success story. I wanted to go to college and make something of myself. I knew I control my own destiny. I was determined not to let my environment effect me like it did my mother and father. I want to make better decision for my life. I recognize the notion that the decision a person make in their present time would affect them for a life time.

I had a mission in life when I turned 18 years of age that was to graduate and go to college. I wanted to be a Child Psychologist. Considering everything I went through I wanted to help children. I also wanted to promote the growth of woman in our society. I wanted women to realize there true beauty. These two goals came from me living in an environment that was so unstable. I really wanted to help woman and children. I knew it was more woman out their like my mother and more children like me stuck in a world of confusion. I wanted very desperately to enrich the lives of others hurting soul likes me. I just grew stronger each day and I was used to all the turmoil I lived in. Entering high school changes your state of mind because you start to think more about your future. I now realize that this was my last stretch of schooling. Your mind began to think about college. During these years I started to focus on me and prayed for my family. I learned to appreciate them and accept them for who they are. I stilled lived in my Aunt J with my cousin Hank, and K.D. We had a lot of fun together my Aunt would make us have family night. Everyone would gather around the table and play spades. My Aunt was a real family oriented person. I learned to forgive my cousin K.D. for what he did and I taught my sister to do them same because he was still family so we had to move on. I and K.D. use to go to the mall a lot one night coming back from the mall I came the closest to death I had ever come. Driving home from the mall my cousin and I made a right turn on this street called University. University had fork in the road where you had two options to go. We always had to go to the right and keep straight. To get the cross streets of Martin Luther King and Featherstone. We lived off of Featherstone the house that I grew up in Pontiac was right across the street from the Silver Dome. We had been coming this way my whole life. I and my cousin was in the car the street was dark at this time it wasn't no street lights. Before we could reach that cross street. I was looking down eating a nacho supreme from Taco Bell. The mood of the car was happy. We were holding a conversation on 2pac death. He just had passed way. Then suddenly a man was in the middle of the street pushing what it looked to be a brown dumpster on the passenger side of the car. My cousin didn't see him because he wore a patch on his right eye because of a prior basketball accident. Before I knew My Cousin white sable hit the man pushing the brown dumpster. The white sable went under the dumpster the man was pushing. I black out from the impact of the car hitting the man and the dumpster. I don't know how long I was out. I heard my cousin scream my name asking if I was okay. I looked at him and responded yeah. K.D. had a big gash on the side of his face with white meat hanging out because his face hit the steering wheel. I just knew that the glass from wind shell hit my face I wasn't sure of my condition because I couldn't see myself. I just knew my face was burning because I had glass fragment in it. My tooth went through my lip. My mouth was busted open. We both got out the car and my aunt was there.

I don't know who called her and how she was there so fast. Our house was 2 min away from the crash site. I stood on the side walk and waited on the ambulance to arrive. While standing there I was able to gain more insight on the crash. I saw the man that was pushing the dumpster. His body was between the white sable and the dumpster lifeless. He died instantly from the hit and was caught between the two items. They moved the dumpster out the way and put him in a body bag. I never saw a dead body before and the sight was awful. I was traumatize my cousin and I had killed somebody is how I felt. Even though he was the one driving I felt guilty. The ambulance drove us to the hospital. My cousin had to get his face stitched up. When I got to the hospital I notice why my face was burning. I went into the bathroom and my forehead was all cut up. The glass destroyed my forehead. My forehead was swollen and bloody. My forehead looked like bloody hamburger meat. I stood in the bathroom and picked glass from my forehead. I also noticed how bad my mouth was. I tooth went through my lips and chipped. It looked like something from a scary movie. This wasn't no movie it was my face. I stood there and cried for a long time. My self-esteem and confidence was lower all at was. Then I went back to the hospital room with they had me. The nurse came in and gave me techna shoot and cleaned all the glass out of my forehead. After the accident my cousin got charged with Manslaughter and serves a jail sentence while he went to work. He became very depressed during this time. I was sad to see him that way. He gained a tremendous amount of weight and wouldn't come out of the bedroom.

Chapter Eleven

I left the Pontiac area after that accident and went to stay with my mother. I wanted my mother to console me. My mother took me to get my tooth fixed. I wanted to get surgery on my forehead to clear the abrasions. The doctor said, "I had Keloid skin so it would probably become worst than it already was." I used creams to help the scar tissue. I really wanted my old forehead back I felt like a monster and very unpretty. Everyone around me would say it not that bad. They weren't the ones with the scars on their face so they didn't know how bad it was. These scars on my forehead really affected me emotional. I didn't know how to live with a scared face. I became depressed again and wanted to die. My mother helped my gain my confidence back, she reassured I was still pretty no matter what was on my face. I began to believe her after a while. Being in Detroit also helped me cheer up. I was back surrounded by love and support from my neighbor friends. My mother addiction at this time wasn't bad at all. She had a job at some factory. She took care of home. My grandfather (Ben) had given her a Baby Blue Cadillac. She took very good care of it. She appeared to be control of her life. My mother best friend gave me a lot of encouragement also. I went to Pershing High School in Detroit I loved it because I wasn't around all the fake people of Pontiac. My attitude changed and I became a social beautiful again. I was happy once again. I wore a smile that stood for happiness and joy and I wasn't hiding any pain inside. I was cool with a lot of people but I had one good friend Trenea. We became very close and still remain close to this day. The beginning of my 9th grade year began with a calamity. I was able to pull through and find some strength. Each time I looked at myself in the mirror I began to feel confident about my forehead. My forehead just didn't matter anymore it was a part of me. I learned how to accept my scars. My grandfather told me the story of how Jesus had rose from the dead. He still had the scars from the nail located in his hands and the whips on his back. That story was amazing. I felt if Jesus had scars than I could have them as well. My lil red sister, had a quote, she said "You can't change nothing that out of your control." This incident was at the beginning of my ninth grade year. I became content with it. During this year living with my mother wasn't bad at all. She was very supportive and she took me to the dentist and to fix my chip tooth. My mother good behavior couldn't last long. She has been a rebel her whole life. This year she was working at some factory in Detroit. She met a man name Eric. Eric was quickly a part of our family. In the beginning Eric was a nice man who appeared to have my mother interest at heart. That was all a fraud. This man was very deceptive, manipulative, and heartless. I never saw a man with so many bad traits. He was anything but nice. In fact he didn't have a nice bone in his body. He didn't live with us. He stayed with his mother. My mother was never at home. She lost her job and began to spend all her time with him and his family. Eric family was full of dysfunction. His mother had a boyfriend and a husband. He father was a nice, gentle, and sweet. I really like him; I couldn't understand how he got mixed up in that ball of confusion. He had a step-brother who I never met and two sisters. One of his sisters had six kids. I couldn't believe that in this day in age one woman would have all those kids and not be married. Another sister had three beautiful daughters but she start having kids at 12 years old. Then my thoughts were how her mother let her have become a mother so early. No one had an educational background. I went to the house one time when I was 14 and never went back. This family didn't have any structure, stability, or self-control. The house had the nasty carpet I ever saw in my life. I don't know what color it was suppose to be but it was black. They had two chow dogs running around. They also had an equine.

The children ran around looking dirty and their hair wasn't combed. At night all the children would sleep on the floor or the Grandmother bed. It was people and children everywhere worst than being in Lansing. The adults would get drunk. I couldn't believe my mother would adapt to such a family. She would stay with them a get drunk every night she was there. One time she was there my sister caught her getting high in the bathroom sorting drugs up her nose. My mother had spent totally out of control in this environment with these people. This family made me realizes that I had a perfect family compared to them. I told myself so what my Aunt is mean she that way because she cares and what me to grow up and be successful. My father wasn't there for me but that didn't matter either. He wrote me every chance he got. He showed he love and affection through a pen and a piece of paper. I knew deep down in heart if he could be there he could. I grew to appreciate my family flaws. My Lansing family wasn't this bad. My father girlfriend had plenty of intellect she just had a drug problem. This family my mother found was a disaster. Nobody in the whole entire family had common sense beside the Father (Charles). I felt he got trick somehow. My mother had really done it this time. I couldn't understand why she would go so low. It wasn't for me to understand. I completely my 9th grade year with honor no support for my mother because she was always with Eric getting drunk my sister and I was struck raising ourselves. I was use to going through chaos by now. It just became normal. I started to focus more on my education and made sure my lil red baby was taking care of. I would get money from my grandfather (Ben) when I went him and grandmother apartment located in downtown Detroit and clean up. Then the money I receive I would buy my lil sister clothes and shoes. Then I started to babysitting people children and I brought our clothes. I started to take care of myself and her. We didn't have anybody. My mother knew I would have money so when she would come home. She would cuss me out and call a lil black bitch and tell me she wasn't going to take my seizure medicine away from me if I didn't give her no money. She would call my sister a lil red bitch and I would stand up to her so my sister did too. She would punch us both in the chest. This would go on for hours with her cussing us out to get the money I had. I would refuse to give it to her. I will tell her she could punch and cuss all she wants. I wasn't giving her a dime. My sister would be crying uncontrollable I would hate to see her cry. My sister would make me give it to her so she would shut up. I really didn't want too. I did so my sister would stop crying. Soon after I gave it to her she would leave us in the house by ourselves. I would hold my sister and tell her it's going to be okay once she leaves. My mother drug habit had turned her into a monster also. She wasn't the woman I knew I couldn't deem that she would act in such a matter. I really felt sorry for her but really for myself. As for me I became numb to the whole situation.

My mother came home one day from the destructive household and she had two big black eyes. The worst I had ever seen. Yes Eric was physically abuse her too. I thought first my father, then Fred and now Eric, what is wrong with this woman? Eric was hitting her just because the sky was blue. He was heartless with his beating. He didn't even give the black eye to heal before he created a new one. He face stayed black and both eyes. It was real sad. During the mist of all this she found out she was pregnant. She was having a boy. My (Tamari) was born in November just like me. I wasn't that happy to get another sibling this time. This situation my mother was in I really didn't want her to have no kids by this man. I had to face the fact she really wasn't a good mother to the three kids she had. I thought to myself this will be another child for me to raise. I had enough of my mother and her confusion. I started to think about my future. I couldn't deal with her drama anymore.

Chapter Twelve

At the age 15 I made the conscious decision to leave my mother home and I went back to Pontiac with my Aunt. Yes my Aunt was still mean. By this time I didn't care how she was. I was just happy to be in a stable environment. My sister didn't follow me I wish she would've. Her and my Aunt didn't get along. My sister didn't tolerate my Aunt behavior. She said, "If she was going to go through bullshit she rather it is her own mother." I really couldn't blame her. I was older and tired of going through the drama with my mother. I was trying to focus on my future. I was thinking about college. I knew my Aunt household was the best place for me if I wanted to have a bright future. My Aunt taught me how to be very responsible I need that structure. She taught me how to pay bills, open up bank accounts, and how to focus on what is important in life.

　　She was mean as hell in between her teaching me the vital skills I was going to need for adulthood. I would go visit my sister almost every weekend. My mother was living in a house that shouldn't been tore down with Eric. Eric would walk around as if he was God gift to women. He had four more children beside the one by my mother. I couldn't understand what women saw in this uneducated fool. He didn't have a job, no future goals, and couldn't provide for his kids. My mother and grandmother took care of the one child he had by my mother. He wasn't even nice looking. He was 6 feet 5 and dark skinned. He facial feature were normal by that I mean all the same size. He was a complete an idiot in my eye. I really want to kill him. He kept my mother face brutalize. Both eyes still black and lips were busted. I was cleaning her wounds in the bathroom when I was visiting one day. I asked why she was taking this. She replied she just wanted to be with one of her kid's daddy. I said,

"At what cost." She couldn't say anything just put her face in her hand and cried. I rubbed her back.

I went back home after that visit and cried until I couldn't cry no more. That I had a horrible dream that Eric had killed my mother. Three months after that visit my mother left Eric. She ended up in the same shelter we were in before we went to Atlanta. My sister had to live in a shelter again with a new baby boy in that little room. I couldn't believe it when I went to go visit them. It brought back so many memories. She was also pregnant again 16 months later with a girl this time living in the shelter. I had a lil sister and wasn't happy about that either. I enjoy my sibling I just didn't enjoy the man she was having her by or the family they were being brought into. She stayed in the shelter into it was time for her to have my new baby sister (Tamia). Then she went back to Eric. When she went back he held her in the room and would beat her for days for leaving him. Her black eyes they were so big her face was unrecognizable.

Chapter Thirteen

At the age of 16, 17 I really can remember because I had the same reoccurring dream every night for years. That dream was that Eric killed my mother. I really felt that deep down in my heart and soul that Eric was going to kill my mother. I couldn't feel anything during these years. My grades dropped I didn't care about anything or anybody beside my sibling. I stop caring about myself and future. I just didn't want a dead momma. I had a lot of sleepless night because I didn't want to have this dream. I wanted to join the high school community and be involved in a lot of activities and display my talents. I couldn't because I was depressed and stress out about my mother. I still visit and on one visit my mother told me that

Eric had another child that was two month young than Tamia. She was so hurt and crying. This man was amazing. He didn't work, not looker, and now a cheater. The other woman had the nerve to call the house and ask for him. He talked to her right in front of my mother face. I had enough with this man. So that night I went into him and mother bedroom and told him how I really felt. I have never cussed at an adult into that night. I called him everything I could think of. This man was so disrespectful that he cuss me back out and told me he would hit me. I told him I wasn't Lisa so bring it on. My mother jump in the middle of us she said, "You can hit me but you can't hit my kids." He walk away as he was walking I called him a crowd and bitch ass nigga. I wanted him to turn around so I could fight him but he didn't. I was angry and frustrated I wanted to take out my madness of him. That night my mother slept in the bed with me and my sister scared to go back in the room with him. He had put her through so much pain. I felt so sorry for her and rocked her to sleep. When I went back home I knew he beat her for me standing up to him. I felt very guilty for doing that. I said to myself if she dies it will be my fault because I should've kept my mouth close.

My brother Quan went through tragedy during these years. He lost his grandmother from cancer and less than a year later he lost he mother due to kidney failure. To add insult to injury before my father went to prison Quan's mother and him had a baby together and they named him after my father. The baby lived for only 4 months and died of crib death. My brother had lost 3 very significant people in his life before the age of 18. I admired his strength during this time. He mourned but in silence. At his mother funeral he got up and walked. Afterward he was appeared to be okay. My brother was my hero because of this. For years I always looked up to him for handling the death with greatest. I admire his strength to move on. I kept thinking to myself he is young but, he handled the death of 3 people so well. My brother and I share the same birthday. Watching him handle adversity reminded me of myself. Most Scorpio endure a lot of pain but we handle is with grace, dignity, and respect.

Chapter Fourteen

At age 18 I pretty much felt the same internally. I knew how to wear a smile on my face to hide the pain. I was happy because it was my last year of high school. I didn't partake in any senior event because I was still depressed. My mother was dying every seconds my Eric. The beaten just got worst and worst. I would still have the same dream every night. It was a very hard time for me I thought for sure Eric was going to kill my mother. I hoped for the best but I prepared for the worst in concerning my mother. I graduated by the grace of God. I felt great because I have accomplished something. When I walk across the stage I felt liberating. I knew that I was done with my bondage of my family. I was going to go into the world and find myself. I told myself after I walk to never look back. I wanted to have a successful future, after I walked across the stage and we through our hats in the air. I went and hugged everybody in my family. Which were my Aunt J, Aunt Tammy, Cousin (K.D.) My grandmother (Ruth) and my red baby sister? My friends from Detroit had come down? To my surprise my mother was nowhere to be found. My first thought was she is dead. I asked my grandmother where she was she told me she didn't no. Then suddenly to she appeared like magic. She was swinging her hands in the sky and running towards me. I was so happy to see her. I burst into tears. I was crying tears of joy because she wasn't dead. Then I looked at her condition. She had two black eyes the size of a grapefruit, two broken finger and a knot at the top of her head. My tears suddenly turned into angry because I knew Eric had done this to her. I was still happy she made it and he didn't kill her. I asked her how she got so beat up. She said, "Eric of course black eyed of eyes that was normal, but then he grabbed a hammer and held her two fingers down and hit them with the hammer. After he did that he hit

94

her in the head with the hammer. My sister saved her life because she ran to a pay phone and called the police. When the police got there Eric went in a closet and hide. The police pulled him out and put him in jail for attempted murder. My mother went through the whole trail process. She explained what he did on the stand. I was proud of her because she actually stood up to him. The prosecuting attorney got the charges reduced. This idiot only did 90 days in jail. I thought "Amazing" the woman has been through so much. After this event she went back into a shelter with 2 more additional children and my red baby. She got a house and job. She was doing well. Considering everything she went through.

Chapter Fifteen

Another event that happened when I was 18 years of age was I lost my virginity. Seem like everybody in my surrounding were having sex. I thought what the hell. I had sex with this boy I had known a while. The relationship wasn't serious but for the most part I was just curious. To me I was late because all my friends lost their virginity early in high school. Here It was had graduated and still haven't done it. I was hearing how wonderful it was. I really didn't have anyone to talk to about sex. My Aunt didn't have conversation like that with me and my mother was getting beat on. So my friends were the only key I had when it came to this subject. They seemed to really enjoy it. This experience was rather weird to me because I really wanted to wait until the right time. Give myself away to my husband. My Grandmother said that what she did. I was trying to walk in her footsteps. She was so a positive force in my life. Nevertheless I had sex. I enjoyed it of course but it wasn't what all my friends made out to be. I and the boy lay in the bed he got on top of me I didn't know rather to fight him or lay there. I felt like he was evading my personal space. I wanted to push him off until his male part met my female part. I thought, okay I get it but it hurt really badly for the first 10 minute or so. I was thinking my cousin Hank is going to kill me. Why I'm doing this but it felt good. I had mix emotions as I laid there. It last it less than an hour. What scared the hell out of me was afterward. I got up and it was blood everywhere. I never saw so much blood in my life. It was very disgusted. I clean myself up. The next day I was excited because I had a sex story to tell my friends instead of listening to their, I didn't leave not details out. Later on that night was the excitement was gone. I felt that I couldn't waited but in reality is really wasn't that exciting. I thought I was pure now I'm dirty just to tell a story how dumb. Sex is not made to tell a story is supposed to be unity between a man and woman to express their love for each other when they are in love and marry. I really didn't like my actions because I knew better. I thought I made a big mistake. This was my first mistake of my life. Then I went into deeper thought. I believe I committed this act because of lack of guidance. I was screaming for attention and trying find so kind of happiness. I was very confused and upset with my dysfunctional family. I used sex as an outlet. I have learned from my first big mistake.

Chapter Sixteen

My brother Pee Wee always stayed on the back of our minds. Once we got of age my sister and I would try to locate him on the computer. We would come up short but wouldn't stop looking. This brought joy to my mother knowing that we were looking for her son. I was always taught that Gods works in mysterious ways. One day God prove that fact. My Grandmother (Mattie Ruth) and my mother went to a credit union that my grandmother had been going to for over 25 years. My grandmother goes in the bank to withdraw some money for grocery shopping. It was on a Friday. She went grocery shopping every Saturday. She was also getting money out to give to my mother for her habit and the kids. My grandmothers enabled her daughters like never before. I believe she love them so much she just ignore their flaws. As she was filling out the withdraw slip. Her teller said, "Grand mama" She looked up and to her surprise it was PeeWee. We hadn't seen PeeWee in 10 years and there he was working at the credit union. My grandmother face was filled with tears and she told him his mother was outside. He asked his boss if he could take a break. Of course his break was granted this situation was very significant. My grandmother brought my brother to the car where my mother was located. Her mouth instantly dropped. Her face was filled with tears also. He gave my mother and grandmother his contact information. He went back to work. My sister and I went to see him the very next day. To our surprise he still looked the same. He grew up in a nice respectful family. His adopted father was preacher. His adopted mother was a nice lady. He told us he bounced around to a couple of foster homes before he found this family. He was with this family for about 8 years. I was so happy to hear he was raised with respect and dignity. He told me and my sister that his family changed his last name. The most amazing thing every is he lived right down the street from our house. He was still in Detroit Mi. We thought he was out of state somewhere. That was the reason we couldn't find him. My mother was the happiest woman alive. For the first time in history she had a since of joy in her eyes. My grandmother cooked a wonderful Sunday dinner for all of us. Our family felt complete again. I was very happy to see that my brother turned out to be a success story. He had a good head on shoulder. He had a clear vision to where he wanted his future to take him. For years we missed him and God put him back into our lives. We always have stayed in contact with him from that day forward. This event occurred the summer before I left for college. Two years later PeeWee went to college 2 hours away from me. PeeWee went to the army then came to school. The army paid for his education. The family was worried when he decided to go to the Army. It was a good move for him at the time. We always stayed in contact at school and the rest of our lives.

Chapter Seventeen

I was born on November 4th 1981 with the umbilical
cord wrapped around my neck. The doctor pulled
me out the womb with forceps. I had a scary way of
coming into this world. Even as a newborn I overcame
the struggles. I came out a healthy and happy baby.
I have been through so many trials and tribulations.
I have many more to tell but, I still remain strong.
I now look back on the first 18 years of my life and
recognize it was all for the greater good. Yes I have
been through it all in these 18 years, but I didn't want
to become a victim of my environment. I wanted to
create a more favorable condition. I wanted to turn
all negative I have witness into a positive energy.
I now know what's important in life. I have live,

learn and grew from my family occurrences, mistakes and downfalls. I appreciate everyone in my family because they made me into the woman I am today. I have learned to love everyone in my surrounding, be grateful for the good and the bad, and take every life experience as a lesson to learn from. I know now that through all trials and tribulations. I was still blessed because it couldn't have been a lot worse. I been though it all but through the grace of God I made.

Be Inspired!

"What's On My Mind?"

There are many thoughts on mind such as; the notion of major corporations failing to provide services because economic hardship, hard-working American people are losing their job security, homes and peace of mind. Men and Women are at a battle with one another within a relationship filled with deception, miscommunication, and no trust or believing in one another.

Though all of this confusion the one vital factor that stand out in my mind is our children are killing one another. The children are dying at the age of 13, 14, and 15 years old. They are dying by the hands of one another. These children are the key to our future. This is very sad because the babies have lost their hope, faith, and respect for one another. They also have no desire for the future. These children have no mentors, family structure, and stability in their lives.

"Now I suggest we come to together as a nation and help our children, because our mere existence is at stake. Everyone Americans has to believe in the concept that it takes a village to raise a child. Take the time out to listen, communicate and understand any child to save our future. That's what on my mind.

"Death"

On May 8, 2009 my cousin Myrun passed. This is
the same day as my brother Peewee B-Day. I woke
up at 6:00 a.m. to wish my brother Happy B-Day
and to tell him to have a blessed day. I went to work
and started my routine day. I got off work at 3:00
p.m. While I was driving home I was thinking about
what food I was going to eat and the present I was
going to get my brother. I pulled in my drive way
around 3:30p.m. I went in the house to search for
food. In the process of this action, my sister called. I
answered and to my surprise her voice on the other end
of the phone was very weaken and shallow. I instantly
became worried because I never heard her sound
this way before. She said, "Are you sitting down."

I said, "No just tell me what's the matter is." She said, "Myrun is dead" I said, "Myrun who", as if I didn't know who she was talking about. She said, "Our cousin." Then I sat down. Everything I was doing or thinking about before that was at a screeching halt. My sister just cried and cried on the other end of the phone. I hung up from her. I was in total shock and disbelief. Then I needed confirmation so I hung up the phone and called my brother and other sister to hear the news two more time. I hung up the phone again only this time I wasn't in shocked any more. I was in pain. The pain was I felt was indescribable. I was totally devastated. In writing this passage I'm still in pain and disbelief. My cousin Myrun died in a car accident at the age of 27 years of age. He had graduate from college with a degree in Computer Engineer. He just brought a son in this world who was only one year of age. I and My cousin were 3 weeks apart in age. Knowing his character as a man made the pain even worst.

Death is a destiny that we all know is coming one day. The questions to ask yourself are; will you be preparing for this unfortunate event? Is there a way to cope when your parents, child, cousin, grandparents or friend pass? There's no definite answer to these questions. I just believe you must be strong and a spiritual person. A person must believe that God knows best. The person who life has ended is at God will, so you can't question his authority. The pain still remains for the remainder of your life. Just know that you must live for yourself and the people around you. Nothing will ever take the pain away. Believe that the person spirit is in a better place. Believe in all the good memory you have and find peace. Keep your love one in your heart even though they aren't here in the physical form they still remain in your spirit. This is how I handle my cousin death.

"How do you cope with death? Stay strong believes in a high power, find peace, tranquility, and pray for healing."

"Let It Go"

Our childhoods are filled with many trial and tribulations. Some are worst than others but the affect is still traumatizing. In order for an adult to prosper they must let go of all the unhappy moment located in their childhood. A childhood memory should be just that a "memory." People must let go molestation, abandonment, and child abuse. Even as an adult you must learn to let go of the people who mistreat you on your jobs, different family members such as in-laws or mother/father.

My personal childhood is filled with abandonment issue by my mother and father because they choose the streets over their children. I also lived with my Aunt who had an evil spirit. She treated me as if she didn't love me. My mother also put one man before me when I was younger also. I had to learn to let go of the treatment I received from my parents and Aunt I learned to accept them for who they are and pray from them.

On my career path their always someone jealous because my work ethnics are different from there's I display more heart and I'm a hard-working. I choose to ignore the ignorant people and walk by faith and not by sight. I know that God has a greater path from me so, I ignore the people who try to stop it and I pray from them too.

"Please don't let your pass determine your future. Don't let people get in the way of your blessing a head. Let It Go and forgive people so you will have a promising future."

Self-Determination

Self-Determination occurs as a baby trying to grasp his/her first step. Then as a person mature through grade school. Confidence, Personality, and Level of Security with one self starts to transpire. Sudden your G.P.A. matter or the goal of becoming a start athletic or top cheerleader all these magnificent effects stem from self-determination.

But somewhere along the way as an adult self-determination is lost. Mainly because life as you once knew it didn't turn out the way you planned or hope for. Some of your family and friends turned not as supportive as they should be. They should be loving, compassion and respectful people. For example, I graduated from college with a degree in

Speech Communications. I found a job working with abused and neglected teenage girls. One day coming home from work. I get a phone call from my little sister she was calling from the neighbor home. She asked if I could pick up her and my little brother because my mother had put them out the house. At this time my sister was 6 and my brother was 8. I went and picked up my sibling and been taking care of them for going on 5 years now. During this time my mother was having a nervous breakdown and on drug heavily. She wasn't maintaining her motherly duties accuracy and their father wasn't anywhere to be found at this time. I also adopted my sibling during the years also. This situation put my self-determination on hold. I was very down because it went from just being me to two kids and me. I quickly figure out a way to take care of two kids, go to school and work.

Don't become selfish, stubborn and insubordinate because the world is an ugly place. Still strive as if you that baby taking it first step. Step with your head lifted high; keep your self-determination going this will open up many doors, even when the doors are slammed in your face.

"Self-Determination is something embedded to promote growth, so please don't lose it.

"Think"

Often times one hear the word think before you speak and think before you commit any action you may do. Think about how your misguide behavior may affect others. Nevertheless we have people who don't think about anything but their own self-gratitude.

We have younger and older women opening their legs to men without any commitment barrier set in place. They open their legs to look for love, security and comfort, Instead of looking inside themselves and finding their inter-peace and beauty. Women need to wake up and think about this senseless act of "sex" is ruining their bodies. Women need to think about their self-worth, believe that they are queen, stop allowing men to abuse and misuse them. Women need to stop and think what they really want out of life, instead of being a playground for men. But stop think that's this issue isn't all the man fault because, a man is only going to do what a woman allows him to do. Women take the time to figure out who you are than the man will follow.

Now I lost my virginity when I was 18 years old. Yes I have had sex with men with no commitment barriers. I stopped and thought about some of my actions before I committed them. Sometime I didn't. I know my self-worth and I stop and think about all my action when it concerns a man. I was also in a mentally abuse relationship for 3 years. Although he wasn't blacking my eyes the mental was worse than the physical. He chocked me twice but he words had more impact on me than him putting his hands on me. I lost two great friendships. He wrecked a brand new car (Pontiac G6) I just got. He destroyed my peaceful spirit, state of mind, and lowers my self-esteem. I had to realize I was worth more than what he was telling me. I left him and I'm single but its beautiful become I had found myself finally. I now know what I want out of life without living in the shadow of a man.

As for the men please stop and think about your families they are creating instead of walking away from them and when they are committing crimes. I often times hear some men say a 9 to 5 isn't for me or college. Men stop and think is 20 years to life for you then. Men wake up and realize that your kings. Treat your women like queens. Think about the how street lives damage your character, hope, and their no future in it, beside dead or in jail. Men stop and think are the hustle ambition really worth it. Men stop and think about the endless possibility that the world has to offer. For the good men who have realized their potential this reaches out to the young men who are lost and confused.

"Men and Women think before you speak, think about your actions and most important think about yourself."

"Don't be an in Enabler"

I recently wrote a letter to my mother to express to her how I felt about her. The letter went in details about her life but at the end of the letter I let her go. The letter went as follows. Mother you have instill something inside me every mother should put in their child. You raised me with a pure heart, talk to me about everything this raise my confidence and awareness, and you taught me to help others and obtain blessing when so do. I really appreciate having you as a mother. You're a one of a kind Lisa B. You're a gift from God. You have some many gift and talents that's amazing. I just wish you saw your many gift and talents the way your 5 kids do.

On August 31, 2009 we lost our Mattie Ruth Nance she was a beautiful spirit. I thank God for putting her in our lives for 84 years. Your mother was just as beautiful as you. She set a great foundation for this family. Now it time to move on and let her spirit rest and let her spirit completely live within you. My grandmother was your backbone and enabler for the majority of your life. She was there for all 5 of your children when you were able to be there. She was there for you during your drugs years. She even gave you money and took you to the drugs house to purchase your drugs. She just did this out of a mother love for a child. Your drugs years were filled with a lost soul and confusion because you couldn't let go of your childhood trauma. That was being mentally and physically abuse by your father. Nevertheless you overcame your drug addiction, your addiction to men abusing you. You a very strong woman and I admire you for that. I have so much love and respect for you. You inspired me to be the best I could be and always gave me the confidence I needed. I believe in you like you believe in me. Now I think it time for you to take your life back. Mother you have developed an addiction to alcohol it's hurting the family just like your drugs did.

Your children want nothing but the best for you. Now you must leave my stronghold and my home to develop the skills, talents and gifts that God gave you. Since I stop enabling my mother she is now doing fabulous and free of her addiction.

"Don't be an Enabler you hurt yourself and the person who you are trying so desperately to save."

"Love"

A four letter word that means so much this simply four letter word is a beautiful method to show affection. Love is supposed to be a deep connection between human being to human being and even deeper love for God. Love is displayed in many different ways. Such as marriage couple shows harmony, unity, and respect with their love. Mother and children love is unconditional. Fist love you in order to love another human being.

Love is often taking out of contexts. Because people don't wait patiently on love they rush love because of no self-control or self discipline. This is when love lost occurs. People find themselves frustrated, depressed, and lonely. Love isn't supposed to leave one lonely, lost or desperate. Love isn't supposed to mistreat or abused.

I have been a victim of verbal and physical abuse because I thought my ex-boyfriend loved me. I stayed with him for 4 years taking harsh treatment. I also witness my mother go through the same treatment. Before I was in a relationship with my ex-boyfriend I had a friends with no commitment barrier put in place I also viewed that as love. I believe this way how love was supposed to go. My terrible attitude and smart mouth didn't help my struggle with love. I learned to be patience and pray for God to seen me someone. In the meantime focus on myself and what important to me.

"People please don't take love out of context. Love yourself and spread love from your heart to everyone even the people you don't want to love. Love everyone and receive a blessing.

"Follow Your Dream"

My Mother once told me that don't anything comes to a sleeper but a dream. If you have a dream of being on the top of the world than pursue that dream. Look at the late great Martin Luther King "Dream.", that dream once so amazing it came true 40 years later. Our forefather has made a path for us to walk into freedom, justice, and serenity, so why not adhere to the dream that's burning on the inside of you. Please don't let life troubles get in the way of your dream. Follow your dream and become an impact on society.

For years I worked with abuse and neglected teenage girls and I also worked in the elderly/disabled community. I have a strong passion for people. I love to help out those who are less fortune. I gain insight on how people lives have lead them down wrong path and I learn for their mistakes. All the while I was working with the teenage girls and elderly/disabled community I was yearning to be doing something else. My inside feeling was telling me to become my own business owner. I have to step away from the community that I loved and had great passion for. I became a proud business owner. I follow my dream that have been sitting there for years. I also always wanted to write a book. I follow my dream and did that as well.

"Follow your dream to become a better you, inspire others also believe in yourself and anything is possible.

"Know and Count Your Blessing"

Many of us don't know our Blessing because our mind is filled with negative thoughts. Know that child being born, a roof over your head, and the ability to have a meal everyday are blessing. Many of us have the desire to want more such as a better career, house or car. But first count the blessing that you already have. Then patiently wait on the other blessing. While you are waiting thank God for the blessing you have already received.

Please remember that God don't put no more on you than you can bear. God put each of us though test to see if we can pass them. Once we pass our test. We are supposed to share our testimony with others to motivate them to do right. Once your test is over your blessing are sure to come. Always be prepare for the next test he is going to be you though. These tests are to make you stronger and appreciate the blessing to come. While you are being tested count your blessing and know the ones you already have.

"Know your blessing; Count Your Blessing, In order to have many more."

"Divine Harmony"

Divine Harmony isn't easy to obtain. These two words together or powerful, divine means godly, marvelous, celestial, and discover. Harmony means an agreement. First one person has to understand how to construct positive, peaceful energy and godly way to doing your actions within themselves then come into an agreement with this new fashion of behavior. People must loose anger that's embedded inside them, Change their negative attitude toward situations that can't be changed, and most vital learn to accept people for who they are and stop trying to bring them down all the time. Promote peace and happiness. I thought if I were to exploit people weakness I was so how helping them because I was making them see what I see. Like telling my mother and father they wasn't their when I was a child because they choose the street over their children. Or telling friends I have lost about all their flaws. When my siblings make an irrational decision I immediately jump down throat. In my relationship with men I really gave them a great deal of tongue thrashing. My wording toward people was very very harsh. I had lost the years of angry and frustrated that was build up for a not so great childhood. I believe I took my pain out on the people around me. I learn to accept the people in my life for what they have to offer and not look down on them. I have learned to promote peace, happiness and understand people when they are faced with unseen circumstances.

"Divine Harmony can be created in one's interior and outer character only when one acknowledge the inner life as a foundation of relentless encouragement for channeling, and shaping his/her outer existence.

"Learn to be Meek"

The power of words can affect a person for a lifetime. People in the modern time really need to watch the word that forms in that mouth. A person doesn't always have to act rude or out of their character when a circumstance a rise they don't like. People need to learn how to be meek or humble so their blessing will come. For instance, as a child a got hit in the mouth on many occasions because I had to have to last word and I would never back down from my mother. Looking back on my behavior if I were to close my mouth I would have had the opportunity to receive more gift and I wouldn't get hit as much as I did. I never realize it wasn't worth it. I have now learned to be meek, watch what I say and respect other people feeling.

"Humble yourselves therefore under the mighty hand of God, that he may exalt you in due time. 1 Peter 5:6

"Have Faith"

Faith is something unseen but it's plays a major part in a mere survival. Faith is in every human spirit each day, when we have faith their calmness in our bones, mind and heart. Despite our shortcoming that come each day if one have faith and believe that these shortcoming will pass then they will. Each day people are faced with debt, current bills need to be paid, and some of us are homeless. Faith ensures us the endless of possible option that the world has to offer. Faith broadens our horizon to know that everything will be okay. Although faith is unseen keep it in your heart and each day will get better.

"Have Faith, Keep Faith and all the good will follow."

"Gain Wisdom"

People seem to think that they are wise because of their accomplishment. Such a bachelor, master, or doctor degree or they are the best in their career fields. They had many plaque and I well known name that have build for them. What they don't realize these are just accomplishments or blessing. These simple achievements don't make a person wise. What a person proves is they are able to make wise decisions. In order to gain wisdom a person need to listen, understand, and communicate with their love one. By doing all this a person heart with open and have balance with the mind. Wisdom will settle in very calming. You may also gain wisdom by your own life experiences. Please learn not to make the same mistake twice.

Another way to gain wisdom is to read. Read books that enhance your knowledge and books that are filled with plenty inspiration. Most important way to gain wisdom is to read the book of Proverbs.

"Pride only breeds quarrels but wisdom is found in those who take advice wise people listen to wise people Proverb 13-10.

10 keys to make your life peaceful

1. Pray every night and every morning on your knees.
2. Get Educated because education is the key to success.
3. Forgive yourself and others for past and present adversity.
4. Be completely honest with yourself and others this will give you a since of peace.
5. Maintain Integrity
6. Save your money and spend your money wisely.
7. Maintain a good health(exercise and eating healthy)
8. Keep a positive attitude and thinking the outcome of being positive is that positive events will occur.
9. Spread love and compassion through your heart.
10. Never lose your ambition.

Quotes from the Bible to
help enrich your life.

"Holding the mystery of the faith in a pure conscience"
(1 Timothy 3:9)

"The tongue that brings healing is tree of life but a
deceitful tongue crushes the spirit" (Proverb 15:4)

"I have learned the secret of being content in any and
every situation whether well fed or hungry whether
living in plenty or in what I can do everything through
him who gives me strength" (Philippians 4; 12:13)

"For in much wisdom is much grief and he that
increaseth knowledge increaseth sorrow" (Ecclesiastes
1:18)

"We also rejoice in our sufferings because we know that suffering produces perseverance, perseverance, character, character and hope" (Rome 5; 3:4)

"Forgetting what is behind and straining toward what is ahead I press on toward the goal" (Philippians 3; 13:14)

"I have come that you many have life and have it to the full" (John 10:10)

"Cast me not away from thy presence; and take not thy holy spirit for me" (Psalm 51:11)

"A greedy man brings trouble to his family but he who hates bribes will live" (Proverb 14:27)

"But the fruit of the Spirit is love, joy, peace, patience, kindness, goodness, faithfulness, gentleness and self-control" (Galatians 5; 22:23)

LaVergne, TN USA
15 October 2010

200859LV00001B/60/P